FEAST OF THANKSGIVING

The First American Holiday

A Play

By June Behrens
Pictures by Anne Siberell

A Golden Gate Junior Book   Childrens Press, Chicago

The author wishes to express her sincere appreciation
to Carol Ramseyer and Jeana Painter,
teachers at Carson Street School, Carson, California,
who directed their students in the first production of
Feast of Thanksgiving

Library of Congress Cataloging in Publication Data

Behrens, June.
    Feast of Thanksgiving, the first American holiday.

    SUMMARY: Recreates the first Thanksgiving as it might
have been, featuring Squanto and a Pilgrim family.
    "A Golden Gate junior book."
    1. Thanksgiving Day—Juvenile drama.
[1. Thanksgiving—Drama. 2. Plays] I. Siberell, Anne, illus.
II. Title.
PN6120.T5B4   812'.5'5   74-3113
ISBN 0-516-08725-8

1 2 3 4 5 6 7 8 9 10 11 12 13 14 15 16 17 18 19 20 21 22 23 24 25 R 75 74

Characters

A PILGRIM BOY
Narrator

A PILGRIM GIRL
Narrator

HOPE
A Pilgrim girl of nine

JOHN
Hope's brother, eleven years old

MILES
John's friend, a boy of ten

SARAH
Miles' sister, age eight

FATHER GOODWELL

MOTHER GOODWELL

SQUANTO
an Indian

RED FEATHER
an Indian boy

Characters

Pilgrim Girl

Pilgrim Boy

Mother Goodwell

Any number of Pilgrims

Father Goodwell

Hope

Miles

Sarah

John

Red Feather

Squanto

Any number of Indians

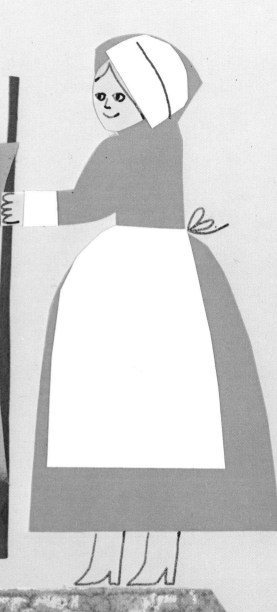

ACT I

The Day Before
The First Thanksgiving,

Autumn, 1621

PROLOGUE

PILGRIM BOY: Over 350 years ago we sailed from England with our parents and friends on the good ship *Mayflower*. We crossed the Atlantic Ocean to the new land of America. We were called Pilgrims.

PILGRIM GIRL: It was wintertime when we reached America. We built houses and started the little town of Plymouth. The winter was long and cold. We had little food. Many of our friends died.

PILGRIM BOY: In the spring, friendly Indians taught us how to plant corn. We learned to hunt and fish. Everyone worked very hard growing food in their gardens and building their homes.

PILGRIM GIRL: In the fall, almost a year after we had landed at Plymouth, there were eleven buildings in our town. The storehouses were full of food from the harvest. We were thankful to be in this new land.

PILGRIM BOY: It was a time for giving thanks. We decided to celebrate with a great feast. We invited our Indian friends.

PILGRIM GIRL: We will take you back to that time. Let's look in on the Goodwell family. It is the day before the great feast.

Curtain rises.
Setting: Inside the Goodwell home.

JOHN: Father, how many wild turkeys did the men get yesterday?

FATHER: The forest was full of wild game, John. We brought back turkeys and ducks and venison. There is a good supply of meat.

HOPE: Oh Mother, the clam stew smells so good! When I see all this food I think of last winter.

MOTHER: Yes, Daughter, you and John went to bed hungry many times.

HOPE: Will there be enough food for everyone tomorrow?

MOTHER: Child, we've been cooking for days. We will have game from the forest and fish from the sea. We have made corn puddings and bread. There are vegetables from the garden. We will have more than enough food for everyone.

HOPE: But not enough for the Indians too?

JOHN: Hope, I think you are worried because the Indians are coming.

HOPE: I wish we could just have our own people. Why do the Indians have to come?

FATHER: Squanto and the other Indians saved our lives. The Indians are our good friends, Hope. We have much to thank them for. We will welcome them tomorrow.

MOTHER: Our friend Squanto helped us through very bad times. Without food and seeds to plant we would have surely starved.

FATHER: It was Squanto who taught us to put a small fish in each hole in the ground when we planted the corn seed. Our corn grew tall and we had a good crop. Now our storehouses are full.

HOPE: How many Indians will be coming?

FATHER: We will know tomorrow.

JOHN: Will they bring their families?

MOTHER: We will *all* share in giving thanks to the Almighty. The feast is for everyone. Hope, do you dislike the Indians, or are you afraid of them?

HOPE: Oh Mother, I *am* afraid of them. They are so fearful looking, and I think they steal from us!

FATHER: Steal? *Never!*

MOTHER: Was that a knock? Hope, please go to the door.

HOPE: It's Miles and Sarah. Come in.

MILES: Good day, Mr. Goodwell. The men are cutting logs for the long tables. They need your help.

FATHER: We will want very long tables to hold all the food the women are preparing.

SARAH: Mrs. Goodwell, Mother needs more bread for the pudding.

MOTHER: I will take the bread now, and help her.

Exit Mother and Father. Miles joins John in shelling corn. Sarah helps Hope prepare the vegetables.

HOPE: I grew these vegetables in my own garden.

SARAH: *Mmmm.* They are sweet and good.

MILES: John, do you think the Indian children will come tomorrow?

JOHN: Mother says the feast is for everyone.

MILES: I wonder if Red Feather will come. Do you remember the Indian boy we met in the forest? He had a red feather in his hair.

JOHN: I will not forget that day. It was the day I lost my ball. Hope and I each brought one special thing when we came to America. Hope brought her little hand mirror and I had my ball. Now the ball is gone. I'll never have another like it.

HOPE: I always carry my mirror with me. I take very good care of it.

SARAH: There is none other in the village like it.

HOPE: John, I knew how sad you were the day you lost your ball. So I went back later to look for it. And I saw the Indian boy again. He picked up something near the edge of the forest. When he saw me he ran away.

JOHN: Is that why you said something to Mother about the Indians stealing from us? Do you think Red Feather took my ball and ran away?

HOPE: I don't know what he picked up. I just thought it might be the ball. I never told you because I wasn't sure.

MILES: Do you suppose he did take your ball, John?

JOHN: I don't know. I saw him in the meadow just a few days ago. I thought he was coming toward me. But when I called out and waved my arms, he ran away.

SARAH: I wonder if he will come to the feast?

MILES: We will find out tomorrow, on the day of thanksgiving.

ACT II

The Day of the Feast

PROLOGUE

PILGRIM BOY: Now it is the special day for giving thanks. The sky is blue and clear. The bright sun shines down on our little village of Plymouth.

PILGRIM GIRL: There are the good smells of cooking over open fires. Women and children are bringing great bowls of food to the long wooden tables.

PILGRIM BOY: Everyone hurries about, doing the last-minute chores. Our guests, the Indians, will be here soon.

Curtain rises.
Setting: A clearing, near the village buildings, where long tables have been set up.

MOTHER: Hope, bring the hot bread. See if the water is boiling in the kettle.

JOHN: I wish the Indians would come. I've been hungry for hours.

MILES: Look, John. Do you see something moving in the forest? I think they *are* coming!

JOHN: Just look at that long line of Indians coming out of the forest!

HOPE: Mother, there are so many of them.

MOTHER: We must let them know we are happy they have all come.

JOHN: There are more of them than there are of us!

MILES: How straight and tall they stand! Look, one is carrying a deer on his back.

JOHN: Miles, there is Red Feather! He is walking behind our friend Squanto.

FATHER: Come, one and all. Let us welcome our Indian friends. Greet them as your brothers and offer them the benches to sit on.

SARAH: There are so many. We don't have enough benches and tables for everyone to sit down.

HOPE: It's all right. Look, some are sitting on the ground.

FATHER: Let us give thanks for our many blessings and pray for a lasting friendship with our Indian friends.

PILGRIMS SING: We gather together to ask the Lord's blessing
He chastens and hastens His will to make known
The wicked, oppressing now cease from distressing
Sing praises to His name
He forgets not His own.

PILGRIM GIRL: When the prayers are over there is great feasting. The bowls of food are emptied and filled many times.

PILGRIM BOY: The Pilgrims and Indians eat the many foods served by the women.

JOHN: Miles, I don't think Red Feather looks like a thief.
MILES: I wish he would look our way.

JOHN: Look, Miles, Red Feather is getting up. He and Squanto are coming over here!

SQUANTO: John, this is Red Feather, He found something in the forest. He tried to bring it to you, but you shouted and waved your arms. You frightened him. He was afraid to come back by himself.

HOPE: Do you mean *he* was afraid of us?

MILES: What is he taking out of that pouch on his belt?

JOHN: My ball! Red Feather found my ball! Oh, thank you, Red Feather. I thought I'd never see it again.

HOPE: It was very wrong of me to think that Red Feather could have stolen John's ball.

JOHN: Do we have anything to give him?

SARAH: I will bring him a bowl of bread pudding.

JOHN: I mean something he can keep. Something to show him we want to be his friends.

MILES: What have we to give? We have nothing.

HOPE: Squanto, I have something to give Red Feather. We want him to know we are his friends. We should not be afraid of each other. This is for you, Red Feather. It is called a mirror.

JOHN (*To Miles*): I didn't think Hope would give up her mirror to anyone.

SQUANTO: Red Feather has great joy in his heart. He is happy with your gift. He wants to show it to his friends.

JOHN: Hope, it was good of you to give up your mirror. Red Feather will treasure it as you did.

MILES: Here comes Red Feather again. He's carrying something. He wants us to come with him to the fire.

JOHN: What are these seeds Red Feather is giving us?

SARAH: They look like corn seeds, but they are so small. Look! Red Feather is putting the seeds on the hot stones.

HOPE: The seeds are popping open. They look like little white flowers.

JOHN: Red Feather is eating them. He wants us to eat them, too.

MILES: *Mmmm.* They're good to eat! Try some, Hope and Sarah.

SARAH: Red Feather has given us a special gift. He has given us a new kind of food to eat.

HOPE (*To Squanto*): Squanto, tell Red Feather that his gift has brought great joy to our hearts, too. It is a gift we will enjoy all our lives.

PILGRIM BOY: There were good feelings between us and our Indian friends.
When everyone had eaten it was time for dancing and games.
PILGRIM GIRL: The Indians danced for us. Red Feather danced best of
all.

PILGRIM BOY: We taught the Indians games and they played with us.

PILGRIM GIRL: For three days we feasted and gave thanks for the blessings of this new land. This was our first Thanksgiving.

Thanksgiving Day, celebrated so long ago by that small band of Pilgrims and Indians on the rock-bound shores of New England, is re-created once again for young children, this time in play form in a book to be read and enjoyed for the story itself or to be easily acted out. The author focuses on a typical Pilgrim family as, in Act I, all prepare for the great feast of the morrow when the Indians, without whom the colonists would surely have perished that first bitter winter, will come to share in the bounty of the autumn harvest. Act II, which colorfully depicts the feast itself, also unfolds a meaningful and ingenious little plot in which the Pilgrim children at last realize that the Indian boy whom they have feared and distrusted is really very like themselves. Charming full-color pictures in collage by Anne Siberell make every page a delight to look at.

JUNE BEHRENS well understands the tastes and preferences of young readers. A reading specialist in the Los Angeles City Schools system since 1965, she holds a credential in Early Childhood Education and has a rich background of teaching experience at all elementary grade levels. A graduate of the University of California at Santa Barbara, with a Master's degree from the University of Southern California, she has written many juvenile books, including *Soo Ling Finds A Way* (a Junior Literary Guild selection, illustrated by Taro Yashima and published by Golden Gate Junior Books in 1965), *How I Feel, Look At Desert Animals, Who Am I?* and other titles for Elk Grove and Childrens Press. The mother of two daughters, she and her husband make their home in Hermosa Beach, California.

ANNE SIBERELL has illustrated a number of children's books for various publishers, including *Who Found America?* and *Lamb, Said The Lion, I Am Here* (both Golden Gate Junior Books). A distinguished woodcut and etching artist as well as a painter, her work has appeared in art exhibitions throughout the country and she has won several awards for her graphics and printmaking. A native of Los Angeles, she received her art training at UCLA and Chouinard Institute of Art. She lives with her husband and three sons in Hillsborough, a suburb of San Francisco.